Three O'Clock Hour
Prayerbook

Arranged and Introduced
by the Rector of
the National Shrine of The Divine Mercy

MARIAN PRESS
STOCKBRIDGE MA 01263

National Shrine of The Divine Mercy
An Imprint of Marian Press
2014

Available from:

National Shrine of The Divine Mercy, 2 Prospect Hill, Stockbridge, MA 01262, 413-298-3931, e-mail: shrine@marian.org

Shrine Gift Shop, P.O. Box 559, Stockbridge, MA 01262, 1-888-484-1112, e-mail: giftshop@marian.org

Marian Helpers Center, Eden Hill, Stockbridge, MA 01263, Prayerline: 1-800-804-3823, Orderline: 1-800-462-7426, Website: www.marian.org

Typesetting: Patricia Menatti

Cover Design: Kathy Szpak

Front Cover: Photo © Marian Fathers of the Immaculate Conception. Courtesy of Marian Archives.

Inside Front and Inside Back covers: Photos © Marian Fathers of the Immaculate Conception of the B.V.M. Courtesy of Marian Archives.

For texts from the English Edition of the *Diary of St. Faustina Kowalska: Divine Mercy in My Soul* © 1987 Marian Fathers of the Immaculate Conception of the B.V.M.

NIHIL OBSTAT:
George H. Pearce, SM
Former Archbishop of Suva, Fiji

IMPRIMATUR:
Joseph F. Maguire
Bishop of Springfield, MA
April 9, 1984

The NIHIL OBSTAT and IMPRIMATUR are a declaration that a book, booklet, or pamphlet is considered to be free from doctrinal or moral error. It is not implied that those who have granted the NIHIL OBSTAT or IMPRIMATUR agree with the contents, opinions, or statements expressed.

ISBN: 978-0-944203-63-7

Printed in the United States of America by the Marian Press.

Table of Contents

INTRODUCTION

I am delighted to share with you the National Shrine of The Divine Mercy *Three O'clock Hour Prayerbook*. Every day, when our bell tower rings in the three o'clock hour, priests and religious, Shrine staff, and pilgrims from throughout the country gather here to open their hearts to our Lord's tender Mercy. We do so in response to Jesus' request as recorded in the *Diary of Saint Faustina*:

> **As often as you hear the clock strike the third hour, immerse yourself completely in My mercy; adoring and glorifying it; invoke its omnipotence for the whole world, and particularly for poor sinners; for at that moment mercy was opened wide for every soul** (1320).

Within this *Three O'clock Hour Prayerbook,* you will find information on the National Shrine and my religious community, the Marians of the Immaculate Conception. Of course, you will also find the Divine Mercy Novena, the Chaplet, and selected prayers we have been using at the Hour of Great Mercy at the National Shrine for well over forty years. It is my hope that this simple prayerbook will be a resource for families and parish communities as they strive to adore and glorify our Lord's omnipotent mercy.

If you have never visited the National Shrine, I extend to you a personal invitation to make a pilgrimage to this holy place. Every day, my brother priests and I offer Holy Mass and provide pilgrims the opportunity to avail themselves of the Sacrament of Reconciliation. At the conclusion of our three o'clock hour Divine Mercy devotions, all religious articles are blessed and pilgrims are provided the opportunity to venerate the relic of St. Faustina.

It is my belief that those who venerate our Lord's mercy have a special place in our Heavenly Father's Heart. Whether you join us at the National Shrine or unite with us in spirit by using the *Three O'clock Hour Prayerbook* in your own home or parish community, it is my sincere prayer that every time you hear the clock strike the third hour you will trust in Jesus even more!

By the Rector of the National Shrine of The Divine Mercy

THE HOUR OF GREAT MERCY
(please read privately)

In His revelations to Saint Faustina, Our Lord asked for special prayer and meditation on His Passion each afternoon at the three o'clock hour, the hour that recalls His death on the cross.

At three o'clock, implore My mercy, especially for sinners; and, if only for a brief moment, immerse yourself in My Passion, particularly in My abandonment at the moment of agony. This is the Hour of Great Mercy … In this hour I will refuse nothing to the soul that makes a request of Me in virtue of My Passion (1320).

As often as you hear the clock strike the third hour, immerse yourself completely in My mercy, adoring and glorifying it; invoke its omnipotence for the whole world, and particularly for poor sinners; for at that moment mercy was opened wide for every soul. In this hour you can obtain everything for yourself and for others for the asking; it was the hour of grace for the whole world — mercy triumphed over justice …

Try your best to make the Stations of the Cross in this hour, provided that your duties permit it; and if you are not able to make the Stations of the Cross, then at least step into the chapel for a moment and adore, in the Most Blessed Sacrament, My Heart, which is full of mercy; and should you be unable to step into chapel, immerse yourself in prayer there where you happen to be, if only for a very brief instant (1572).

From these detailed instructions, it's clear that Our Lord wants us to turn our attention to His Passion at the three o'clock hour to whatever degree our duties allow, and He wants us to ask for His mercy.

In *Genesis* 18:16-32, Abraham begged God to reduce the conditions necessary for Him to be merciful to the people of Sodom and Gomorrah. Here, Christ Himself offers a reduction of conditions because of the varied demands of our life's duties, and *He begs us* to ask, even in the smallest way, for His mercy, so that He will be able to pour His mercy upon us all.

We may not all be able to make the Stations or adore Him in the Blessed

Sacrament, but we can all mentally pause for a "brief instant," think of His total abandonment at the hour of agony, and say a short prayer such as "Jesus, mercy," or "Jesus, for the sake of Your Sorrowful Passion, have mercy on us and on the whole world."

THE NOVENA TO
THE DIVINE MERCY

On Good Friday, 1937, Jesus requested that Saint Faustina make a special novena before the Feast of Mercy, from Good Friday through the following Saturday. He, Himself, dictated the intentions for each day. By means of a specific prayer she was to bring to His Heart a different group of souls each day and thus immerse them in the ocean of His mercy, begging the Father — on the strength of Jesus' Passion — for graces for them. (See 1209.)

Since Saint Faustina was commanded to write down the novena, Our Lord must have intended the novena to be used by others, too. Once published, it immediately became very popular, and people prayed the novena, not only in preparation for Mercy Sunday, but at other times as well. The wide range of intentions, which do not include personal needs, makes the great popularity of this novena all the more astounding. In this novena, we truly make the Lord's intentions our own — a beautiful expression of the Church's privilege and duty, as the Bride of the Lord, to be the intercessor at Christ's side on the throne of mercy.

THE DIVINE MERCY CHAPLET

In 1935, Saint Faustina received a vision of an angel sent by God to chastise a certain city. She began to pray for mercy, but her prayers were powerless. Suddenly, she saw the Holy Trinity and felt the power of Jesus' grace within her. At the same time, she found herself pleading with God for mercy with words she heard interiorly:

Eternal Father, I offer You the Body and Blood, Soul and Divinity of Your dearly beloved Son, Our Lord Jesus Christ, in atonement for our sins and those of the whole world; for the sake of His sorrowful Passion, have mercy on us and on the whole world (476).

As she continued saying this inspired prayer, the angel became helpless and could not carry out the deserved punishment. (See 474, 475.)

The next day, as she was entering the chapel, she again heard this interior voice, instructing her how to recite the prayer that our Lord later called "the Chaplet." From then on, she recited this form of prayer almost constantly, offering it especially for the dying.

In subsequent revelations, the Lord made it clear that the Chaplet was not just for her, but for the whole world. He also attached extraordinary promises to its recitation.

Encourage souls to say the Chaplet which I have given you (1541) **... Whoever will recite it will receive great mercy at the hour of death** (687) **... When they say this chaplet in the presence of the dying, I will stand between My Father and the dying person, not as the just Judge but as the Merciful Savior** (1541) **... When this chaplet is said by the bedside of a dying person, Divine Wrath is appeased (restrained), unfathomable mercy envelopes the soul, and the very depths of My tender mercy will be moved for the sake of the sorrowful Passion of My Son** (811) **... Priests will recommend it** [the Chaplet] **to sinners as their last hope of salvation. Even if there were a sinner most hardened, if he were to recite this chaplet only once, he would receive grace from My infinite mercy** (687) **... I desire to grant unimaginable graces to those souls who trust in My mercy** (687) **... Through the Chaplet you will obtain everything, if what you ask for is com-**

patible with My will (1731).

The Divine Mercy Chaplet is an intercessory prayer that extends the offering of the Eucharist, so it is especially appropriate to use it after having received Holy Communion at Holy Mass. It may be said at any time, but our Lord specifically told Saint Faustina to recite it as a novena prayer during the nine days before Mercy Sunday (the first Sunday after Easter). He then added:

By this Novena, [of Chaplets before the Feast of Mercy] **I will grant every possible grace to souls** (796).

EUCHARISTIC EXPOSITION

O saving Victim op'ning wide
The gate of heav'n to man below!
Our foes press on from ev'ry side;
Thine aid supply, Thy strength bestow.
To Thy great name be endless praise,

Immortal Godhead, one in three;
Oh, grant us endless length of days
In our true native land with Thee. Amen.

O salutaris Hostia
Bella premunt hostilia,
Quae caeli pandis ostium:
Da robur, fer auxilium.

Uni trinoque Domino
Sit sempiterna gloria,
Qui vitam sine termino
Nobis donet in patria.
Amen.

AT THE HOUR OF GREAT MERCY — 3:00 P.M.

SAINT FAUSTINA'S PRAYER FOR SINNERS

O Jesus, eternal Truth, our Life, I call upon You and I beg Your mercy for poor sinners. O sweetest Heart of my Lord, full of pity and unfathomable mercy, I plead with You for poor sinners. O Most Sacred Heart, Fountain of Mercy from which gush forth rays of inconceivable graces upon the entire human race, I beg of You light for poor sinners. O Jesus, be mindful of Your own bitter Passion and do not permit the loss of souls redeemed at so dear a price of Your most precious Blood. O Jesus, when I consider the great price of Your Blood, I rejoice at its immensity, for one drop alone would have been enough for the salvation of all sinners. Although sin is an abyss of wickedness and ingratitude, the price paid for us can never be equalled. Therefore, let every soul trust in the Passion of the Lord, and place its hope in His mercy. God will not deny His mercy to anyone. Heaven and earth may change, but God's mercy will never be exhausted. Oh, what immense joy burns in my heart when I contemplate Your incomprehensible goodness, O Jesus! I desire to bring all sinners to Your feet that they may glorify Your mercy throughout endless ages (72). Amen.

DIVINE MERCY NOVENA

FIRST DAY *"Today bring to Me ALL MANKIND, ESPECIALLY ALL SIN-NERS, and immerse them in the ocean of My mercy. In this way you will console Me in the bitter grief into which the loss of souls plunges Me."*

Most Merciful Jesus, whose very nature it is to have compassion on us and to forgive us, do not look upon our sins but upon our trust which we place in Your infinite goodness. Receive us all into the abode of Your Most Compassionate Heart, and never let us escape from It. We beg this of You by Your love which unites You to the Father and the Holy Spirit. **Eternal Father,** turn Your merciful gaze upon all mankind and especially upon poor sinners, all enfolded in the Most Compassionate Heart of Jesus. For the sake of His sorrowful Passion show us Your mercy, that we may praise the omnipotence of Your mercy forever and ever. Amen.

SECOND DAY *"Today bring to Me THE SOULS OF PRIESTS AND RELIGIOUS, and immerse them in My unfathomable mercy. It was they who gave Me strength to endure My bitter Passion. Through them as through channels My mercy flows out upon mankind."*

Most Merciful Jesus, from whom comes all that is good, increase Your grace in men and women consecrated to Your service, that they may perform worthy works of mercy; and that all who see them may glorify the Father of Mercy who is in heaven. **Eternal Father,** turn Your merciful gaze upon the company of chosen ones in Your vineyard — upon the souls of priests and religious; and endow them with the strength of Your blessing. For the love of the Heart of Your Son in which they are enfolded, impart to them Your power and light, that they may be able to guide others in the way of salvation and with one voice sing praise to Your boundless mercy for ages without end. Amen.

THIRD DAY *"Today bring to Me ALL DEVOUT AND FAITHFUL SOULS, and immerse them in the ocean of My mercy. These souls brought Me consolation on the Way of the Cross. They were that drop of consolation in the midst of an ocean of bitterness."*

Most Merciful Jesus, from the treasury of Your mercy, You impart Your graces in great abundance to each and all. Receive us into the abode of Your Most Compassionate Heart and never let us escape from It. We beg this grace of You by that most wondrous love for the heavenly Father with which Your Heart burns so fiercely. **Eternal Father,** turn Your merciful gaze upon faithful souls, as upon the inheritance of Your Son. For the sake of His sorrowful Passion, grant them Your blessing and surround them with Your constant protection. Thus may they never fail in love or lose the treasure of the holy faith, but rather, with all the hosts of Angels and Saints, may they glorify Your boundless mercy for endless ages. Amen.

FOURTH DAY *"Today bring to Me THOSE WHO DO NOT BELIEVE IN GOD AND THOSE WHO DO NOT YET KNOW ME. I was thinking also of them during My bitter Passion, and their future zeal comforted My Heart. Immerse them in the ocean of My mercy."*

Most Compassionate Jesus, You are the Light of the whole world. Receive into the abode of Your Most Compassionate Heart the souls of those who do not believe in God and of those who as yet do not know You. Let the rays of Your grace enlighten them that they, too, together with us, may extol Your wonderful mercy; and do not let them escape from the abode which is Your Most Compassionate Heart. **Eternal Father,** turn Your merciful gaze upon the souls of those who do not believe in You, and of those who as yet do not know You, but who are enclosed in the Most Compassionate Heart of Jesus. Draw them to the light of the Gospel. These souls do not know what great happiness it is to love You. Grant that they, too, may extol the generosity of Your mercy for endless ages. Amen.

FIFTH DAY *"Today bring to Me THE SOULS OF THOSE WHO HAVE SEPARATED THEMSELVES FROM MY CHURCH, and immerse them in the ocean of My mercy. During My bitter Passion they tore at My Body and Heart, that is, My Church. As they return to unity with the Church My wounds heal and in this way they alleviate My Passion."*

Most Merciful Jesus, Goodness Itself, You do not refuse light to those who seek it of You. Receive into the abode of Your Most Compassionate Heart the souls of those who have separated themselves from Your Church. Draw them by Your light into the unity of the Church, and do not let them escape from the abode of Your Most Compassionate Heart; but bring it about that they, too, come to glorify the generosity of Your mercy. **Eternal Father,** turn Your merciful gaze upon the souls of those who have separated themselves from Your Son's Church, who have squandered Your blessings and misused Your graces by obstinately persisting in their errors. Do not look upon their errors, but upon the love of Your own Son and upon His bitter Passion, which He underwent for their sake, since they, too, are enclosed in His Most Compassionate Heart. Bring it about that they also may glorify Your great mercy for endless ages. Amen.

SIXTH DAY *"Today bring to Me THE MEEK AND HUMBLE SOULS AND THE SOULS OF LITTLE CHILDREN, and immerse them in My mercy. These souls most closely resemble My Heart. They strengthened Me during My bitter agony. I saw them as earthly Angels, who will keep vigil at My altars. I pour out upon them whole torrents of grace. Only the humble soul is capable of receiving My grace. I favor humble souls with My confidence."*

Most Merciful Jesus, You yourself have said, "Learn from Me for I am meek and humble of heart." Receive into the abode of Your Most Compassionate Heart all meek and humble souls and the souls of little children. These souls send all heaven into ecstasy and they are the heavenly Father's favorites. They are a sweet-smelling bouquet before the throne of God; God Himself takes delight in their fragrance. These souls have a permanent abode in

Your Most Compassionate Heart, O Jesus, and they unceasingly sing out a hymn of love and mercy. **Eternal Father,** turn Your merciful gaze upon meek souls, upon humble souls, and upon little children who are enfolded in the abode which is the Most Compassionate Heart of Jesus. These souls bear the closest resemblance to Your Son. Their fragrance rises from the earth and reaches Your very throne. Father of mercy and of all goodness, I beg You by the love You bear these souls and by the delight You take in them: bless the whole world, that all souls together may sing out the praises of Your mercy for endless ages. Amen.

SEVENTH DAY *"Today bring to Me THE SOULS WHO ESPECIALLY VENERATE AND GLORIFY MY MERCY, and immerse them in My mercy. These souls sorrowed most over my Passion and entered most deeply into My spirit. They are living images of My Compassionate Heart. These souls will shine with a special brightness in the next life. Not one of them will go into the fire of hell. I shall particularly defend each one of them at the hour of death."*

Most Merciful Jesus, whose Heart is Love Itself, receive into the abode of Your Most Compassionate Heart the souls of those who particularly extol and venerate the greatness of Your mercy. These souls are mighty with the very power of God Himself. In the midst of all afflictions and adversities they go forward, confident of Your mercy; and united to You, O Jesus, they carry all mankind on their shoulders. These souls will not be judged severely, but Your mercy will embrace them as they depart from this life. **Eternal Father,** turn Your merciful gaze upon the souls who glorify and venerate Your greatest attribute, that of Your fathomless mercy, and who are enclosed in the Most Compassionate Heart of Jesus. These souls are a living Gospel; their hands are full of deeds of mercy, and their hearts, overflowing with joy, sing a canticle of mercy to You, O Most High! I beg You O God: show them Your mercy according to the hope and trust they have placed in You. Let there be accomplished in them the promise of Jesus, who said to them that during their life, but especially at the hour of death, the souls who will venerate this fathomless mercy of His, He, Himself, will defend as His glory. Amen.

EIGHTH DAY *"Today bring to Me THE SOULS WHO ARE DETAINED IN PURGATORY, and immerse them in the abyss of My mercy. Let the torrents of My Blood cool down their scorching flames. All these souls are greatly loved by Me. They are making retribution to My justice. It is in your power to bring them relief. Draw all the indulgences from the treasury of My Church and offer them on their behalf. Oh, if you only knew the torments they suffer, you would continually offer for them the alms of the spirit and pay off their debt to My justice."*

Most Merciful Jesus, You Yourself have said that You desire mercy; so I bring into the abode of Your Most Compassionate Heart the souls in Purgatory, souls who are very dear to You, and yet, who must make retribution to Your justice. May the streams of Blood and Water which gushed forth from Your Heart put out the flames of Purgatory, that there, too, the power of Your mercy may be celebrated. **Eternal Father**, turn Your merciful gaze upon the souls suffering in Purgatory, who are enfolded in the Most Compassionate Heart of Jesus. I beg You, by the sorrowful Passion of Jesus Your

Son, and by all the bitterness with which His most sacred Soul was flooded: manifest Your mercy to the souls who are under Your just scrutiny. Look upon them in no other way but only through the Wounds of Jesus, Your dearly beloved Son; for we firmly believe that there is no limit to Your goodness and compassion. Amen.

NINTH DAY *"Today bring to Me SOULS WHO HAVE BECOME LUKEWARM, and immerse them in the abyss of My mercy. These souls wound My Heart most painfully. My soul suffered the most dreadful loathing in the Garden of Olives because of lukewarm souls. They were the reason I cried out: 'Father, take this cup away from Me, if it be Your will.' For them the last hope of salvation is to run to My mercy."*

Most Compassionate Jesus, You are Compassion Itself. I bring lukewarm souls into the abode of Your Most Compassionate Heart. In this fire of Your pure love let these tepid souls, who, like corpses, filled You with such deep loathing, be once again set aflame. O Most Compassionate Jesus, exercise the omnipotence of Your mercy and draw them into the very ardor of Your love, and bestow upon them the gift of holy love, for nothing is beyond Your power. **Eternal Father,** turn Your merciful gaze upon luke-warm souls who are nonetheless enfolded in the Most Compassionate Heart of Jesus. Father of Mercy, I beg You by the bitter Passion of Your Son and by His three-hour agony on the Cross: let them, too, glorify the abyss of Your mercy. Amen.

THE DIVINE MERCY CHAPLET

You expired, Jesus, but the source of life gushed forth for souls and the ocean of mercy opened up for the whole world. O Fount of Life, unfathomable Divine Mercy, envelop the whole world and empty Yourself out upon us (*Diary*, 1319).

O Blood and Water which gushed forth from the Heart of Jesus, as a fount of mercy for us, I trust in You (*Diary*, 84). (3 Times)

The Our Father*

V. Our Father, Who art in heaven, hallowed be Thy name. Thy kingdom come; Thy will be done on earth as it is in heaven.

R. Give us this day our daily bread; and forgive us our trespasses as we forgive those who trespass against us; and lead us not into temptation, but deliver us from evil. Amen.

The Hail Mary

V. Hail Mary, full of grace. The Lord is with thee. Blessed art thou among women, and blessed is the fruit of thy womb, Jesus.

R. Holy Mary, Mother of God, pray for us sinners, now and at the hour of our death. Amen.

The Apostles' Creed*

I believe in God, the Father almighty,
Creator of heaven and earth,
and in Jesus Christ, his only Son,
our Lord, who was conceived by the
Holy Spirit, born of the Virgin Mary,
suffered under Pontius Pilate,
was crucified, died, and was buried;
he descended into hell; on the third day
he rose again from the dead;
he ascended into heaven, and is seated at
the right hand of God the Father almighty;
from there he will come to judge the living
and the dead.
I believe in the Holy Spirit, the holy
catholic Church, the communion of saints,
the forgiveness of sins, the resurrection of
the body, and life everlasting. Amen.

*From the *Roman Missal* approved for English-speaking countries.

Using the beads of the five decades of the Rosary, pray:

On the OUR FATHER BEADS

V. Eternal Father, I offer You the Body and Blood, Soul and
Divinity of Your dearly beloved Son, Our Lord Jesus Christ,

R. in atonement for our sins and those of the whole world.

On the HAIL MARY BEADS

V. For the sake of His sorrowful Passion,

R. Have mercy on us and on the whole world.

In conclusion: Holy God, Holy Mighty One, Holy Immortal One, have mercy on us and on the whole world. (3 Times)

CLOSING PRAYER

Eternal God, in whom mercy is endless and the treasury of compassion inexhaustible, look kindly upon us and increase Your mercy in us, that in difficult moments we might not despair nor become despondent, but with great confidence submit ourselves to Your holy will, which is Love and Mercy itself. Amen.

A PRAYER FOR DIVINE MERCY

O Greatly Merciful God, Infinite Goodness, today all mankind calls out from the abyss of its misery to Your mercy — to Your compassion, O God; and it is with its mighty voice of misery that it cries out: Gracious God, do not reject the prayer of this earth's exiles! O Lord, Goodness beyond our understanding,Who are acquainted with our misery through and through and know that by our own power we cannot ascend to You, we implore You, anticipate us with Your grace and keep on increasing Your mercy in us, that we may faithfully do Your holy will all through our life and at death's hour.

Let the omnipotence of Your mercy shield us from the darts of our salvation's enemies, that we may with confidence, as Your children, await Your final coming — that day known to You alone. And we expect to obtain everything promised us by Jesus in spite of all our wretchedness. For Jesus is our Hope: through His merciful Heart as through an open gate we pass through to heaven (1570).

Benediction Hymn

Bowing low, then, offer homage
To a Sacrament so great!
Here is new and perfect worship;
All the old must terminate.
Senses cannot grasp this marvel;
Faith must serve to compensate.

Praise and glorify the Father
Bless His Son's life-giving name,
Singing Their eternal Godhead,
Power, majesty and fame,
Offering Their Holy Spirit
Equal worship and acclaim. Amen.

Tantum ergo Sacramentum
Veneremur cernui,
Et antiquum documentum
Novo cedat ritui;
Praestet fides supplementum
Sensuum defectui.

Genitori genitoque
Laus et jubilatio,
Salus, honor, virtus quoque
Sit et benedictio:
Procedenti ab utroque
Compar sit laudatio. Amen.

The Divine Praises

Blessed be God.
Blessed be His holy Name.

Blessed be Jesus Christ, true God and true Man.
Blessed be the Name of Jesus.
Blessed be His Most Sacred Heart.
Blessed be His Most Precious Blood.
Blessed be Jesus in the Most Holy Sacrament of the altar.
Blessed be the Holy Spirit, the Paraclete.
Blessed be the great Mother of God, Mary most holy.
Blessed be her holy and Immaculate Conception.
Blessed be her glorious Assumption.
Blessed be the name of Mary, Virgin and Mother.
Blessed be St. Joseph, her most chaste spouse.
Blessed be God in His angels and in His saints.

Holy God, We Praise Thy Name
Ignaz Franz, 1719-1790. Trans, by
Clarence Walworth, 1820-1900

Holy God, we praise Thy Name!
Lord of all, we bow before Thee;
All on earth Thy scepter claim,
All in heav'n above adore Thee;
Infinite Thy vast domain,
Everlasting is Thy reign. Amen.

La Coroncina
della Divina Misericordia
(usando la comune corona del rosario)

Prima:

il Padre Nostro, l'Ave María,
il Credo

Sui grani del **Padre Nostro**:

Eterno Padre, Ti offro il Corpo e il Sangue, l'Anima e la Divinità del Tuo dilettissimo Figlio e nostro Signore Gesù Cristo in espiazione dei nostri peccati e di quelli del mondo intero.

Sui grani dell' **Ave Maria**:

Per la Sua dolorosa Passione, abbi misericordia di noi e del mondo intero.

Infine tre volte:

Santo Dio, Santo Forte, Santo Immortale, abbi pietà di noi e del mondo intero. *(Diario, 476)*

Preghiera finale:

Dio eterno, la cui misericordia è inesauribile, rivolgi a noi uno sguardo di bontà e moltiplica in noi la tua misericordia, affinchè, nei momenti difficili non ci perdiomo d'animo e non smarriamo la speranza, ma, con la massima fiducia, ci sottomettiamo alla tua santa volanta la quale è amore e misericordia. *(Diario, 950)*

Koronka do
Miłosierdzia Bożego
(do odmawiania na zwykłej cząstce różańca)

Na początku:
Ojcze nasz, Zdrowaś Maryjo,
Wierzę w Boga

Na paciorkach Ojcze nasz:

Ojcze Przedwieczny, ofiaruję Ci Ciało i Krew, Duszę i Bóstwo Najmilszego Syna Twojego, a Pana naszego Jezusa Chrystusa, na przebłaganie za grzechy nasze i świata całego.

Na paciorkach Zdrowaś Maryjo:

Dla Jego bolesnej męki miej miłosierdzie dla nas i świata całego.

Na zakończenie trzy razy:

Święty Boże, Święty Mocny, Święty Nieśmiertelny, zmiłuj się nad nami i nad całym światem.
(Dzienniczek, 476.)

Modlitwa końcowa:

O Boże wiekuisty, w którym miłosierdzie jest niezgłębione, a litości skarb jest nieprzebrany, wejrzyj na nas łaskawie i pomnóż w nas miłosierdzie swoje, abyśmy w chwilach ciężkich nie rozpaczali, ani upadali na duchu, ale z wielką ufnością poddali się woli Twojej świętej, która jest miłością i miłosierdziem samym.
(Dzienniczek, 950)

La Coronilla
a la Divina Misericordia
(rece la coronilla usando el ranto rosairo)

Comience:

un Padre Nuestro, un Ave María,
y un Credo

En las cuentas del **Padre nuestro**:

Padre eterno, Te ofrezco el Cuerpo y la Sangre, el Alma y la Divinidad de Tu amadísimo Hijo, nuestro Señor Jesucristo, como propiciación de nuestros pecados y los del mundo entero.

En las cuentas del **Ave María**:

Por Su dolorosa Pasión, Ten misericordia de nosotros y del mundo entero.

Para terminar, tres veces:

Santo Dios, Santo Fuerte, Santo Inmortal, ten piedad de nosotros y del mundo entero *(Diario, 476).*

Oracion final:

Oh Dios eterno, en quien la mi-sericordia es infinita y el tesoro de compasión inagotable, vuelve a nosotros Tu mirada bondadosa y aumenta Tu misericordia en nosotros, para que en momentos difíciles no nos desesperemos ni nos desalentemos, sino que, con gran confianza, nos sometamos a Tu santa voluntad, que es el Amor y la Misericordia misma *(Diario, 950).*

Le Chapelet
à la Miséricorde Divine
(on récite le chapelet sur un rosaire ordinaire)

Au début:

Notre Père, Je vous salue Marie,
Je crois en Dieu

Sur les grains de Notre Père:

Père Éternel, je T'offre le Corps et le Sang, l'Âme et la Divinité de Ton Fils bien-aimé, Notre Seigneur Jésus-Christ, en réparation de nos péchés et de ceux du monde entier.

Sur les grains de Je vous salue Marie:

Par Sa douloureuse Passion, sois miséricordieux pour nous et pour le monde entier.

A la fin trois fois:

Dieu Saint, Dieu Fort, Dieu Éternel, prends pitié de nous et du monde entier. *(Petit Journal, 476)*

Prière finale:

Dieu éternel, dont la miséricorde est insondable et le trésor de pitié inépuisable, jette sur nous un regard bienveillant et multiplie en nous Ta miséricorde pour que dans les moments difficiles nous ne désespérions ni ne perdions courage, mais que nous nous soumettions avec grande confiance à Ta sainte volonté qui est l'amour et la miséricorde-même *(Petit Journal, 950)*.

THE CONGREGATION OF MARIANS OF THE IMMACULATE CONCEPTION OF THE MOST BLESSED VIRGIN MARY

The Congregation of Marians was founded in 1673, when Stanislaus Papczynski left one religious community to found another dedicated to Mary, the Immaculate Conception. Papal approval for the new community came in 1699 when the Holy See permitted the Marians of the Immaculate Conception to make profession upon an existing and approved rule consonant with the name and purpose of the Marians: the Rule of the Ten Evangelical Virtues of the Blessed Virgin Mary.

The new community grew quickly, perhaps not only because it was the first clerical order founded in Poland, but also because it was founded by a man of peasant origin, and accepted men of peasant origin into its priestly ranks. But as history attests, when a founder dies, the community often undergoes fiery tests. External and internal conflicts arose. War, pestilence, poverty, and the lack of discipline all took their toll on the young order, and the subsequent, almost unending, political upheavals in north central Europe, Italy, and Portugal almost destroyed the Order.

In 1909, Blessed George Matulaitis, with the permission of Pope Pius X, secretly revived the Order when it had dwindled to only one member. He opened a House of Studies in Fribourg, Switzerland, to avoid the political persecutions in Czarist-dominated Eastern Europe.

The numbers grew, and in 1913 the first official house in the U.S.A. was opened in Chicago to serve the spiritual needs of the Polish and Lithuanian immigrants. In 1944, the Marians purchased the Eden Hill property to establish a novitiate. Four years later, the St. Stanislaus Kostka Province was officially established, with its headquarters on Eden Hill.

The Marian Fathers of the Immaculate Conception are the founders and custodians of the National Shrine of The Divine Mercy.

For information about the Marian Fathers of the Immaculate Conception, contact the Vocation Director or visit our website, www.marian.org.

NATIONAL SHRINE OF
THE DIVINE MERCY

In 1950, the Marians of the Immaculate Conception asked 74 year old Antonio Guerrieri, a local wood-carver and self-taught designer and builder, to build a church adjacent to the former mansion of the Field family, now the Divine Mercy Residence.

The exterior of the Shrine, large blocks of marble and granite originally quarried in Lee, are from an early powerhouse on the former Westinghouse estate in Lenox. The interior of the Shrine is the work of local wood-carvers who, under the direction of Mr. Guerrieri, worked on site making the beautiful panels, arches, and delicate carvings.

The murals were painted by Joseph Amato of Bridgeport, CT. The stained glass windows, depicting scriptural scenes that portray God's mercy, were the work of Fred Leuchs, a local, nationally known artist. The wood-carved statues of the twelve apostles on the wall behind the main altar are the work of a family in northern Italy. The wood carving of Saint Faustina was made by the same Austro-Italian family and represents her mission to the world. The Stations of the Cross are from Spain. The rose window on the back wall is made up of symbols of Our Lady and required more than 2000 pieces of glass to fabricate.

The icon of the Risen Christ, enthroned above the main altar in a mandorla of gold rays, symbolizes the glorious manifestation of The Divine Mercy in the person of Jesus Christ, from whose pierced side God's Great Mercy emanates upon all humankind.

The beautiful white statue of Our Lady, the Immaculate Conception, represents the titular patroness of the Chapel and the Congregation of Marians, custodians of the Shrine. The side chapels contain intricate stained glass windows of Our Lady of Czestochowa and Our Lady of Ostra Brama, attesting to the Congregation's original ministries to Lithuanians and Poles in the United States of America.

With the exception of some interior changes over the years, the Shrine remains today as it was completed in 1960. From the earliest days, pilgrims have come to bask in the mercy radiating from the image of Jesus, The Divine Mercy Incarnate. On March 20, 1996, the Bishops of the United States declared the Shrine of The Divine Mercy a National Shrine.

Another Book and a Video from the Shrine

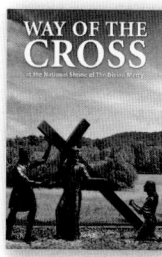

Way of the Cross
At the National Shrine of The Divine Mercy
Introduced by the Rector of the National Shrine of The Divine Mercy

This perfect-bound book is the newly-revised, expanded Way of the Cross commemorating the Blessing of the life-size Stations of the Cross at the National Shrine of The Divine Mercy. It contains St. Faustina's Way of the Cross (compiled from the *Diary of St. Faustina* and Scripture) and the Traditional Way of the Cross based on the version by St. Alphonsus Liguori. In addition, fourteen meditations — one for each Station written by Marian Priests and Seminarians, provide insightful reflections on Christ's Passion. Additional articles and photo-spreads make this book a keepsake and a reminder of Christ's Passion. Book, 80 pages. **CWY3**

The Chaplet of Divine Mercy
in Song Live from: the National Shrine
of The Divine Mercy
Produced by Trish Short in Collaboration with the Marians and Eucharistic Apostles of The Divine Mercy

Here is a contemporary, fresh version of the Chaplet of Divine Mercy — a prayer that pleads God's mercy on the whole world. This sung version opens with a slow, graceful piano that leads to a crescendo with guitar and percussion. As the melody builds and the background vocals blend in, the Chaplet turns into a soaring, heartfelt prayer imploring heaven for God's redeeming love. This Chaplet was filmed live at the National Shrine with the goal of sharing this urgent message of mercy with people of every background, faith, and culture. DVD, 26 minutes. **DMSDVD**